Young Galaxies

Poetry

Abigail George

Mwanaka Media and Publishing Pvt Ltd,
Chitungwiza Zimbabwe
*
Creativity, Wisdom and Beauty

Publisher: *Mmap*
Mwanaka Media and Publishing Pvt Ltd
24 Svosve Road, Zengeza 1
Chitungwiza Zimbabwe
mwanaka@yahoo.com
mwanaka13@gmail.com
https://www.mmapublishing.org
www.africanbookscollective.com/publishers/mwanaka-media-and-publishing
https://facebook.com/MwanakaMediaAndPublishing/

Distributed in and outside N. America by African Books Collective
orders@africanbookscollective.com
www.africanbookscollective.com

ISBN: 978-1-77931-481-9
EAN: 9781779314819

© Abigail George 2023

DISCLAIMER
All views expressed in this publication are those of the author and do not necessarily reflect the views of *Mmap*.

ii

Dedication

To Mikale and daddy

Table of Contents

A prose poem Introducing Young Galaxies

All poets are cosmic drunkards. The name of this book came about from paying attention to experience and intention, notes and scribbling and the putting together of words. My brother has a breakfast joint, the lunch joint, the dinner joint and the after dinner joint while I long for a drink. I have never had children and never got married. I am a writer and poet. People know my name in certain circles or not at all. I am a daughter and sister. Nothing much else I guess to write home about. I lived for a time in Johannesburg with my aunt and her adult son, then at a shelter in Hillbrow and had a stint at a psychiatric hospital Tara H. Moross Hospital in Johannesburg. I was doing a rain dance around my siblings and my parents. A dance of tears, aloneness, forlornness and sadness. My father begins the day with his spectacles perched at the end of his nose reading. Always reading. It's Christmas 2022 and I am finishing this book. My mother is baking up a storm in the kitchen. The dogs have long solemn faces. I am in my room curled up under a blanket in the fetal position. I am in the mood for a samosa. Breaking up the parcel of fried spinach and salty feta cheese in my mouth. I want to be happy but I don't know how to be happy. That's my problem I suppose. I don't have those tools. That skill. I have never acquired them in my lifetime. I must prepare, I feel, for the rain dance of my depression. It's the season.

There are days when I feel nothing. As if I'm a cosmic irritant. When my mother says nothing to me as I sit on my father's bed across from her. I feel as if I am this cosmic irritant when I help my father out of the shower and towel dry his naked body. Do my parents know what this makes me feel like? I painfully want to make conversation with my mother. She has never said for all of my life that she loves me or is proud of me. We've never had that love language. What she has been is over critical, patronizing and condescending. She has behaved in underhanded ways towards me, and has been resourceful in doing this and I have carried a torch for her my entire life. I have loved her from afar and near, up close and personal. I spend a lot of my time alone now. When I was in my twenties working at a production company I longed for a solitary life. There are some parts of me that want to be absorbed into a crowd, that want an otherness kind of life around me. I have always wanted to be loved. The day is hot. I sit in the sitting room and wait for a man that will never appear again in my life. I think of the beauty of that interlude in my life. The touch of his hand on my back, a finger stroking my knee, his arm around my shoulder as he pulled me in close and kissed me. I didn't know anything, flustered sometimes I didn't know how to respond. I don't long for him now as I did a year ago. I want to forget the woman I became in that time and space. Today it is hot. The dogs are melting in this heat. They've eaten larvae that were in their water bucket. Are dogs always hungry for anything? I think of the vagrant who got an erection when I gave him peanut butter bread with coffee. I think of high school and the season. When my dad would buy us season tickets for the swimming pool. We were like dolphins in the water. I think of my time in Johannesburg when I was homeless and still going to film school. I think of the invasion of ticks on my dogs.

I like liquor. I like to drink. I drink alone. Sips of beer. Orange juice mixed with a tot of vodka. Deliciously cold going down my throat. I remember my aunt downing beers on a daily basis. Throwing them back like there was no tomorrow. Until the day

2

she died. The sour effervescent taste of the cold beer at the back of my throat. I want to be happy so much but something keeps holding me back from its threshold's meeting point. My brother bought four bottles of beer. The green bottles were cold. One was empty. The remaining bottles were half full. I looked at it with longing, and such joy and happiness filled my heart. I didn't want to think about my father asking me if I had a high sex drive and did I ever go to brothels in Hillbrow? There was a shelter in Hillbrow that I stayed at for a time. A place for abandoned women and children. Yes, I was abandoned. I had come to know it as a way of life. Being neglected, abandoned and abused. I am numb. I think of free radicals. I think of politics. I think of handsome poets and the stink in the kitchen coming from the sink of dirty dishes piled high. I think of my mother screaming at me to clean up the sitting room where I built a fort with my nephew. How these days all she can do is scream at me. I think of how I have never found love or how love has never found me only sexually depraved men who exploited and took advantage of me and saw to it that their own needs were met. My life has been very sad and so lonely. Loneliness fills the rooms of my childhood home, a manic depressive father and a sad and elegant mother. As a child I was obsessive, a compulsive over achiever in the face of hostile authority figures and in the face of a dominant mother, meek father. Now I learn things about myself all the time. My silence also has a voice and its own timeline. My father has controlled me all his life. My mother neglected me. Every morning and evening she gives me pills. Pills to sleep and tranquilizers when it is time to go to bed. When it is morning she's up and at it with vitamins for tiredness and my vitamin deficiency, pills for my blood pressure, my thyroid, a water tablet for my chronic kidney disease, my mood stabilizer for my bipolar. Perhaps I deserve this. I have to pay for my mentally ill sins. But there are other days when I am writing and the world is an undeniably beautiful place and all seems alright with my place in it. I have a rather imperfect personality. I am rather tired of being sick, meeting relapse after recovery, I am tired of being tired, I am tired of this bipolar shadow hanging over me. Of having never been invited to weddings. There have been funerals but I don't know how I will act, respond, react so I don't attend them. I think of my family and how I get no response from them. How they want to put me in a facility, a psychiatric home. I write of how I wish at this moment (but I know it will pass) for death to come and how I want it to be easy.

How I want to be happy. I will it through imagination. My brother's fiance has put the ultrasound of their child on her WhatsApp profile. I think of the Salinger short story "To Esme, With Love And Squalor". How it's become a dream to turn it into a short film but with a South African undertone. I doubt anybody's life is perfect and beautiful most days. I have lost people along the way. I've lost interest and they've lost interest. I think of an editorship position I held. The excited phone calls when I had been up all night with no sleep but how soon I slowly stopped functioning. Stopped sleeping. Then there was the proposal but I'd rather not speak about that. The absolute squalor of that experience. Two years ago before lockdown I was in a state of happiness. Two years later I am rebuilding my life. I am coping. There was a man who had been in the picture but he isn't anymore.

I began not caring about anything. This morning, most mornings, I have lost the will to survive. I began to not care about my father especially. His conversation began to turn to sex with me more often. He wanted to escape. So did I. But I had my chances. I had escaped to Swaziland and from there I wanted to go to the London Film School but after I returned home Christmas my father hid the letter from St Mark's telling me I had been accepted for A Levels. I was completely devastated. My life has been a struggle and perhaps if I had just taken a chance on love whenever the opportunity had presented itself I would have been alright.

Break, break, break. When it came it was like a knife in the air. A steak knife, butter knife, did it matter? There was something so fatalistic about it. Omg, I was so young. I was just a baby. Mental, mental, mental. This chord runs through me. The name calling (I know how relatives see me), the stigma, seeing things that weren't there, delusions, paranoia, hospitalization and hallucinations, hearing voices. My depression is something like a rain dance. I am a writer, an author of books, a short story writer, essayist, poet and all that I have achieved is marked by depression.

I am sixteen years old, thin and artistic. I stare at my teacher from my desk. He wears thin shirts. He's unmarried. He's published a book for schoolchildren. All of these notes of information I store them up as I come to learn of them through rumors and schoolgirl gossip as I do my secret love for my English teacher. He takes the bus and every day he can be found in a thin stream of schoolchildren walking from school to the center of town, construction all-around of a parking lot. His fingers are the fingers on a guitar. So, his words become my words. Everything about him is electric. Remembering how futile everything seemed to be in the beginning when I had first found myself in this country. Swaziland. How miserable and homesick I had been, it had all been worth it.

In my mind's eye in the time he takes with the short story he reads aloud with expression and the questions he poses to different students, while he walks around the class I devour the characters and the lines of poetry he recites like a flame. He constructs fire, cats, young love, symmetry, sleet beautifully. It is almost as if I can feel the young heroine's passion. I am that young heroine cast aside in youth, that most high feeling not reciprocated, not given a chance to develop, transition into maturity. Secret love crushed, just a seductive experiment, a material concept for my wish-fulfillment ideals.

There are molecules in everything. Even in sir's feats of pretty things he left behind when halfway through the school year he disappeared on me leaving all of us half-smitten schoolgirls with our skirts hiked up high, brushing against thigh, knees quite bare and long-sleeved white blouse, dark heads bowed over their readers, textbooks and binders behind. There was no warning that he would leave to teach at another school. So, it was something that took me by surprise when the new English teacher introduced himself. And I had to learn how to cope all over again.

Stars far off were whirling away at a swift glance with a pure, pale rush on this sleeping planet. Loss I learned bound you, the beautiful, the fragile and the rare and in the swan-like wonderland of this ancient countryside I remembered playing with dolls, the wounds children would leave behind that mushroomed, exploded like torture and that was slow to vanish. I melt into the river of darkness all around me in my dreams in this foreign country. (Swaziland is a swimming goddess on the end of my mother tongue, all I want to do is translate it), darkness like a decorative shroud covers me up from view until it seems I can hardly breathe but it is for my own good. It is to protect me from witches, vampires and werewolves, zombies and the apocalypse. No more Mr Smith to protect me.

The other learners are more unforgivable yet less conniving and wild than other girls and boys I've come across. There was part of me that was scared of growing older, celebrating another birthday, going through with the ceremony of all of that. All my life I've been, well, frightened what other people would think of me. So, this is where my conversations with Buddha and God come in. I found in silence a song of love and the older I seemed to get the more that song seemed to give way to a theory of flight and I simply came alive to see what escape there was in it.

Like shooting stars falling from the night air's skies orbit to the earth, they do not journey gently in dreams. Mr English, K.R. is still three suns exploding in my face and in his leave of absence I found that there could be a continual sense of healing found. Healing multiplied in name, identity, space and peace of mind. When he was no longer there, I would pretend I was writing to him in class, that he would get my letter and that I could touch the fine-fine threads of his silver hair, trembling, that I could run my hands through it, through my fingers, pinch his unkempt hair. I would write to him in equations, promising solutions, graphs that could be negotiated, essays, assignments. I knew, I knew that no relationship would ever come of it.

I was still a relatively young girl on that stretch of open road reaching emotional maturity, a spiritual existence, a sense of my physical being and the sense of the more experienced, less giving world around her. And that I was as present as present was present. I did not yet know that as a woman I would-be capable of many wonderful things in my future. I did not know then that I would become a writer. That the wisdom I collected in youth would only be put to use later on in life. I had no idea that that high school stage would pass, like the age of 16. It was a world that I didn't quite feel up to the challenge of taking head on, made up of chiefs and tribes of men that I didn't feel I completely belonged to naturally.

Sir made me wish to be united against this world with someone who could speak for me, protect me against the harsher, darker elements, harmful dimensions. I was depressed but I didn't call it *depression* then. Then I called it 'being quiet, being slow, soaking up the sun, sucking hollows into warm chocolate Easter eggs melting in my hands, dreaming of the syllables unfolding in my imagination of haiku. In Swaziland, everyone knew that I was weird-different and in accepting that I was different took the shape of the Nile.

I finger the bottle. I think I am going to have that drink after all. I can feel the sour effervescent coldness in my mouth, as it slides towards the back of my throat and I swallow. In that moment I felt such a sense of freedom. The dogs need to be fed and I get up, make my cup of tea first. A cup of black tea. I leave it on the kitchen table to get cold. So it will be at room temperature when I come back inside. I have alcoholics in my family. On both the maternal and paternal side. My mother likes stout. She would hide the bottles in her wardrobe under blankets and clothes. We'd find it as children and laugh and pretend to drink out of imaginary bottles and then we'd stagger around. Did Hemingway have beer for breakfast? Then I must be in good company.

Beer for breakfast, beer first thing in the morning, that's the behavior of an alcoholic, isn't it?

The retired psychiatrist

He remembers hearing
The words we
Are not couples
That fight all
The time. He looks at his wife who
Is not speaking
To him. We are
Who we are. And
Thinks to himself
That the sea
Is tired. Perhaps
As forlorn as he
Is. He's a man
In the garden. He imagines
The sun covering
The dark water.
Cold to the touch.
He wonders what
The right language
Of love is for winter guests. How
To make peace

With his wife. He wants to embrace
Her. Take her
In his arms as if
She was a girl
Again. Brush her
Hair out of her
Face with his granadilla
Hands. Forget

That he is in the
Autumn of his
Years. He wants
To forget that he
Used to do this for a living.
He wants to know if his unhappy marriage is on
The verge of
Cracking up.
He wants to know
If she's finally going to leave him.

Your slender neck

I make the telephone
Call even though
I don't really want to.
I search for cool words, the right language.
I'm searching
For you but
You're difficult
To find. You're
Not on any map
And every road
Is covered in darkness
I imagine you (the golden breakthrough of you)
The golden light
Of you that is
Only found in a museum.
You're a woman
Now. No longer a girl.
Of all of you
That is so necessary to me for me
To live and think of

While I live and
Work in another city.
This is what
I want to say.
You're so beautiful.
Blood a rock face.
Twin flesh making me giddy
You make me weak.
There's a music school

12

Inside my head.
I think of you sitting
Down or washing
The dishes. Eating
A simple meal
Never understanding
How much I love
You. How much
I need you in my life.
Your voice is
Tender and sweet on the other end of the line.
Your flame is bright.

Swimming towards emptiness on a bright summer day

The unforeseen visitor
Emptiness, like blood
Can be graceful and intelligent.
Poured into the
Human body it can be
Useful. You can
Gather it in your
Arms, call it, all the cells and platelets, 'harvest'.
But be careful because
It can come with the
Mechanism of wild gestures.
It will remind you that you need your
Rest after a lover
Has left you high and dry.
It will make you
Shake it off like a fish.
You will find yourself
Swimming towards it on a bright
Summer day without
A care in the world.
The mansion of the sky on fire. Life tired
Of the heat and dust.

Emptiness will be on
Your tongue. It will be
Your mother tongue
Until a replacement comes
Along. Another migration
Will take place. You will
Fall in love again.

You will learn to live again.
It will happen when
You least expect it though.
When your country is tired
Of being broken by waves.
Of being cold or tired.
Of being called 'meat country'.
Or the exit. Or the escape. Or even so quiet
That it is terrifying.

Watching everything through a blur of tears

I never went to
my aunt's funeral.
Although I loved
her very much.
I couldn't cope
with the grief of
losing her. Of never
seeing her again.
All I have is our conversations in the dark.
Her fragile life.
Her life, her life, her life.
Nothing ordinary
about her. Her
standing in the kitchen barefoot.
I think of writing

Her name in the
Sand every time
I go to the beach.
It will mean something to me.
Like the word 'spirit'.
It will take away
The waves of regret
I sometimes feel
Of not going. Of not saying goodbye properly.
She's ashen, salt,
And light. The key
To her soul a sword
In the same way
The pen that I feel in

My hand is to me.

Alone in my grief stricken sadness

Shy daughter, I want her to say
I never wanted you
To have abandonment issues. I never wanted you
To talk about our relationship
To a psychotherapist
Or write about how I
Never wanted you.
All I want her to say is three words
I love you not even
I love you most of all
Or I love you best just
Three simple words: I love you. And two more words
You're mine and five
More words I have
Always wanted you, and three more for
The darkness of this open road called life
You were wanted.

Having a beautiful mother, growing up, and not being beautiful in that way

Once there was a country

I called that country 'childhood'.
The seashore is just a sugared waterfall.
The blue day a confetti of
Wasted sweetness. I have no use for water.
No use for tears. Having a
Beautiful mother, Growing up and then
Not being beautiful in that way made me
Braver. It gave me courage.
I know what immortality is.

The day's spirit is made of
An autumn chill and rain. The change
In the environment a small inheritance.
Daylight's geography is a blood knot.
I am lost and found again in the tired sea of
That difficult, empty country. Once,
I knew what love was, what to call
That personal velocity, that speed
But now I am at the end of the world.

Once there was a country

I called that country
'Childhood'. The seashore
is just a sugared
Waterfall. The blue
day a confetti of
Wasted sweetness.
I have no use for water.
No use for tears.
Having a beautiful mother, Growing
up and then not
being beautiful
in that way made
Me braver. It gave
me courage. I know
what immortality is.

The day's spirit
is made of an autumn chill and rain.
The change in the
environment a small inheritance.
Daylight's geography
is a blood knot. I am
lost and found again
in the tired sea of
That difficult, empty
country. Once, I knew
what love was, what to call that
personal velocity,
that speed but now
I am at the end of the world.

The future language of silence

I have a secret double life.
My eyes are
Sad. The glass
That I am
The Drink is half empty.
I've been set free.
This is me
Saying goodbye
To you. The
Vision of all of wishful thinking you.
In ways that
Were prophetic.
For a while it was magic.
There are still

Some good people
In this world. So remember me.
Staring back at
You close enough to finger distant
Places of war.
The knowledge of
Sticky glitter like
Honey on my
Hands. I'll forget
That you left me broken inside.
All I want is
For you to hold me like
You need me.

The trauma

I let it fall in the dark
After you kissed
Me I went weak.
Weak in the knees.
What kind of emergency was it?
The emergency that
Took you away
From me. When you returned you said nothing
Of the trauma. So I made it up
As we went along
The school of break up.

The day you left
Me the juice of the river was a mothering
Kind of a ghost.
Its tongue had all
the answers I was
looking for. Pigeon feathers catching the light.
I am an authority
On you. The equilibrium
You give me pure
And cool lake-water. I want to forget
You. Your flight.

After all it was
just a game. I still
Want to touch
Your face. It's hopeless. Touch.
You're the feat, the fear, the high. You're life.

I'm caught up.
With pace, time,
Climate, change,
Place. I'm in a
time machine. I'm from yesterday, today and tomorrow.
You're long gone.

Distance lends enchantment to the view

You're art even
Though you're
Broken. Once you were the most beautiful thing
I had ever seen
in my life. A masterpiece meant only for my eyes.
Light fills me.
Light fills even you.
I need you to call
Me beautiful. I need you to say
That I'm perfect for you.
That I am lovely.
That I'm the girl
Of your dreams
But I know that
You won't really mean it, will you.
The words aren't there.
You just want to go all the way with me.
That's the only
Thing I'm good
For, isn't it. For
Your river, meat, flesh.
For your blood, skin,
Yellow hair, rough hands.
Your hair is golden
In my hands. I say, yes,
Yes, yes, yes, yes, yes
Because my heart and I are both
Lovesick and hurt.

The haunting love letter to the bone woman

See here, here is the pomegranate chamber
Of the man who
Goes by the name
Of Yunus, in the
Flesh. He is lost in translation.
As wet as leaves.
As snow in winter.
The bone woman
Has salt at the back
Of her throat swiftly
Marking its position
Sinking its shark
Teeth into tanned
Strangers at the beach you know so well.
The beach from
Childhood that you swam in.
Stain frozen in time,
Pain, suffering a satellite language.
Youth excites the man.
A whisper is a sign of intimacy.
He's a ghost that
Haunts. That haunts.
His mouth is like
The open mouth of the whale that swallowed
Jonah. It's amnion.

Notes from the universe

Are you still in love with ghosts, treasure hunters?
Ghosts in the wild.
You've found a soul mate
To settle down
With. You're nothing but a dream.
My wilderness. A history, fibre
Safely put away.
But you're no longer
Within my reach.
The lines on your
Face don't bother
Me, and neither does
The gray in your hair.

To touch your skin
Is not why I sin.
Gulf, these streets are paved with flame
The lessons of an
Extraordinary machine
A collective of false security. My nerves
Pass for fire. You're
So small now that you pass for the recovery period
From a sickness.
You're not my husband.
You're my hurt. My
One regret. My bitterness.
My depression.

The experience of love everlasting

There's something unspoken
About the language
Of psychiatry like
The ballad of sitting
In a cafe drinking a coffee.
Observing wives
And husbands with
Their children. Ghost
Stories, love stories,
Hurt stories that come to you like waves.
There's a river here.
Inspiration for a novel
Or a short story there.
People seem to dance
And spin around your never ending.
They make you remember
The years of silence
Between your parents
That you endured as a child.
The face of love your
Mother never gave you.
The experience of love
That men gave you in return
For your silence.

The design of human relationships is so intricate

The nightmare
of my brother
Never gives up.
We all wait up with him until he falls asleep.
Until we all know
That we are safe.
That no harm will come to us
Before or after
Midnight. He usually
Turns the television
Low but that doesn't
Fool any of us.
He walks up and down
The passage. He's cursed.
My brother, my brother
Is cursed. He's
Unemployed. He
Says all he wants
Is a job. Security
For his family but

He is a pretty liar. All
He wants to do with
His mouth is to feed
Us pretty lies mostly.
I think it's all his
Fault. His frustration
Is his fault. He is
To blame for his

Own disappointment
In life. Nobody
That I know turned
Him into an addict.
Every day we wake
Up and he is still fresh,
Alive, and new. It's
Slowly killing all
Of us. I don't love
Him anymore. It hurts
Too much anyways.

The afterlife of stars

We bond over coffee. He 'orders'
me to make French toast.
I stand in the kitchen
watching him through the window.
He's perfect. The egg a
yellow parachute. Dripping into the pan.

Where the ocean meets a lottery ticket

Exile child hard to get
without love medicine.
He's with someone much
More suitable now. Her
body history wilderness. Her
thinking celestial. She preps
the house around him.
In the looking glass you won't find tired
oblivion there or purgatory.

Where the ocean
meets a lottery ticket.

The blessing in disguise

This vision of the
shore. I am left
to admire the sea-view.
Foam, white, blossoms.
They multiply. Many
are still going to die in this flood.
Many have died in this flood.
Where is his armor?
Where is his coat
his hat, his gloves?
Why does he not look
dashing next to his bride?
He does not love
her to death. He loves another
that's why.

The ankle-deep footprint left behind in the sand

Assia Wevill. She's kissed
on the mouth.
Wears my clothes
while I am spirit. I can no longer
hold my children
close. Every
thing, possession's
love story is
a ghost story.
There's a rumor
going around. We are water.
We are life.
Once love poured
out of me. Writing
most of all.

There's a-winter in his yellow hair

I know what abundant freedom is.
I found it there
in your yellow
hair. The moral
compass of love
is so basic. The canvas
itself is ready
to be covered
by the shroud
of the manifesto of life.
I want to write about fear.
We live with
terror everyday
in society's flux.
Even anxiety
must have the
gift of dignity.
I don't want to forget the sweetness
Of your face.
Or give it up to the moon.

After the silence of wearing a Hawaiian shirt

After leaving Johannesburg
I wanted the city
to still resonate
within me but all
I had on my side
was silence.
I craved the early
morning traffic.
Coffee. The people.
I behaved badly.
Life seems long
when you're young.
I spend nights
watching cricket with dad.
The bond still there.
Nobody tells you
about the greatest
secret of love.
That it will change
the way you
see yourself.

On the fingers and lips of your lover

You. Like the
horror-filled darkened howl
of the city
streets at night.
It belonged
to me. Made me feel
whole. I gathered
wisdom in my hands.
It felt surreal. My
mouth dry. My spirit
warm. I have to embrace
the future. This,
this means war.
Now I know what
love is. Letting go.
Letting go.
Health reasons
dictate the distances
I travel now.

The song of the river

Today I find myself in a forest.
I walk in circles
Always coming to the river's edge.
Found the mountain.
Everything was cold.
The day was cold.
It felt to me as if the world
Was awash in snow.
With every footstep I took.
Branches slick. Wet.

No Hawaiian shirts for you cousin

Vincent-pa. The waves silence you now.
Wasn't I good to you?
You promised me
a cassette player once.
Moved away. Married
an Indian girl from Lenasia South.
Salt and light out.
The day's mistress.
Cool propaganda.
The sky is on fire.
Flames licking the nape of my neck.
The sand is warm.
At first under my feet.
Then wet when the
Ocean has washed it clean.
Inside I feel raw, set free.
I love you. I loved you.
Then and now this is my song.
A stone boat on a shelf
Exploding into view. Can you
Hear my voice? My heart is open.
When I was a child I did
What I liked. My thoughts
Were those of a child.
The blue skies are bright. Paradise.
The warm sun on my skin.
The light blinding. Exploding into view.
This is life. Once I loved you.
Now there is only the exchange between

The exits of uninspired pain
And sorrow.

Now there is only paradise.

Untitled

That's loneliness. What was familiar was this.
Pain. Intense. Every
Measure of pain was intense.
Pain that was familiar.
A numb feeling.
If this holiday could
make her happy
Then nothing else could.
If it was in our power
to make her happy then so be it.
There was a mist
hanging as if suspended
from nothing but the air.
It seemed white was obliterating everything
Golden in sight.

Acceptances and rejection letters

You're a prophet
I've willed into life.
Your sweater smells of rain.
You make me
think of Paris.
Once I was in love with you.
That was when
I was a girl.
Foolish with windswept hair
when I came into
class almost breathless.
I was very passionate
about the ideas
I had. You still
remember her.
You still remember
that girl and that
fact haunts me.
Causes me pleasure,
pain, suffering.
I'm somewhat of a nomad now.
Living from city to city.
Coast to coast.
The sky is the limit.
You buy my books.
You read them.
You're something
beautiful, you know.

When I hear my uncle's voice on the telephone

My uncle's voice
is a sheet of glass.
He means to renovate my soul.
When he speaks
I drift away. He
Believes in gardening at night.
He's always lived
in the city. His beautiful wife died of breast cancer.
I couldn't cope
when I heard the
News. So I wrote
this poem instead.
They had three sons.
Too successful.
Is there such a thing as having too much
Success. Women
haven't inherited
them yet. Children.
Mustn't life have
a purpose. Doesn't
having a family or being in
the family way mean
having a purpose? I'm
very much alone now.
Oh, I didn't go to the funeral, and we haven't
spoken in what
Seems like years.

When light poured into me at the swimming pool

There was a sweetness
to this day. The horizon
a blue harsh line. I looked
for stars but there were
none. For some reason
they were always invisible
during the day. My heart
was filled with honey.
I licked the edge of that
spoon clean. I thought mostly
about writing love poems
to myself. I thought about
the history of my chronic illness.
The tartness of jam.
My sadness was obstinate.
It did not want to go away
no matter how many lengths
of the pool I swam.
Stroke for stroke never ultimately
reaching the end. I swam
until my hands felt like
clay. My face soft. I kept on
saying to myself that
the death of the day was a myth.
I make it a habit to fold
my dreams into myself.
My goals, the poetry I write.
I worship this, this light that
Is pouring into me now.

When the mania hits

I am a shadow of my former self. I begin
To have Lilliputian selves. They arrange
Themselves like chess pieces. Ready
For battle. Ready for anything. My hair
The branches of a weeping willow tree.
Branches that have a life of their own.
That could have been called Medusa
In a former life. My savage lungs are flawless.
To breathe is a gift. Summer is a furnace.
Winter is fire. It is strange to me that
Daylight never forgets anything. I am
A screen door. I am driftwood. And then
I begin to paradigm shift everything
In my heart's veins and in every brain
Cell. I pretend I'm happy when I'm
Not. I blame my mother when I should
Be blaming myself. I hate the world.
I hurt and I hate. I cry and I laugh. The
World is beautiful, lovely, all that jazz

But if it is I can't see it. It doesn't fill
Me up with the fizz of joy. Joy always
Begins with the birth of a choice.
I am a sleeping woman. I take to my
Bed. My giant feet, hands are cold as Lake Tanganyika.
I say my prayers that I'm grateful I'm
Not a parent. It's as if something inside
Of me is poisoned. I am no good for
Anyone. Can't move my feet. Can't dance.

Depression always has the landscape
Of winter. It is always summer when
The mania hits. A sultry day that doesn't
Know if it is coming or going. I cannot
Wait for the return to autumn season. Then too,
I am a shadow of my former self. I am
Ready for anything. Every year or so
I pretend to be interested in the ghost that
Wears a veil and a shroud that haunts
Me.

The manic depressive daughter
(for my 'Johannesburg' family)

The furniture is there but it also isn't there.
What I am seeing is not real. It's
like the memory of water's hiding
place inside a lake. Fire for eyes. Moth
wings for limbs. Milk flowing
through bones. All rage and sadness
standing at attention finding them
Instead of the fluid emptiness in a vessel. You are
my sun. All feelings shatter the sunset.
The dawn in ravishing intervals. You
have to see it the way that I see it. That
I am damaged. That the people I have
loved have damaged me. My face, the
Reflection in the bathroom mirror, is a
Museum. It speaks volumes. Grief is
like silence. It has its own soul. I only
had to learn how to love myself and

then all this sadness would end. Rage
would find the exit out. Some escape.
This voice within me has no ending, only
a beginning. You're asleep so you don't
remember. The stillness that came
after the hunger. The forest. The earth. Gravity.
Most of all the red path of the volcano.
Haunted, so the night swimming began
in earnest. I used water to trace vertebrae.

45

I praised asylum. I exalted the keys that came
with freedom. I was a fossil but knew
nothing of choice. I knew what touch
was and in the end longing for it almost
destroyed me. In the end I tried to live up to your
expectations.

The winter rain of Johannesburg

I never had to think too much
of the deep sleep of the moon,
the sun, the stars' ancient airs
and graces. When rain fell from
the sky. The blue reward of
the sky was usually very determined
to hold nothing back like a
fisherman's net cast over that
ethereal element of seawater. Catching
fish came with the stormy perspective
of the day filled with thunder
and lightning. The sea's vast
eternity. The flowers in the garden are
so clear with poise. The wind
is so polite. So parental. The stars swimming
in their own black river. The
skyline's first instinct is to furiously
dissolve with every sunset.
Silence both threatening and
bewildering bouncing off the walls,
bending in the air, flexing its
fluid muscle. Silence is found
there at the end of the world
in an abyss. Our invincible conversations still haunt me. I
never had to think too much of the
deep sleep of the moon, the sun
and the stars' airs and graces.
I remember her kindness. Her
beautiful, open face. She's gone
but not forgotten. She left three

sons and a husband behind. Her
cancer is gone but not forgotten.
Her hair like black silk down
her back is gone but not forgotten.
Nothing complex, complicated
nor intellectual about her. This
salt of the earth woman with her
bright shining eyes marking me
for life and in the letting go
of it all came the lines of poetry.
Showing up at first, all harsh on
the blue lines of the page. She's up there now. Singing
with the angels. Riding the clouds.
Every silver lining her playground.
The only time I ever found
mysticism, faith and love in
one place was in poetry. In writing about
Jean and her cancer's remission.

Winter leaf and the smell of apples

I prefer being the madwoman
In the attic. A Mrs Rochester.
I understand that kind of life.
It pleases me. I can't turn my
Back on it. Walk away from it.
I've already forgiven you. It's
My thing. This a modern way of thinking
On blue days. When the flame of
My soul is on fire. And fasting
The inner music of my soul, the
Night away and old world nostalgia.
You were the one (big magic).
You're still young at heart. Your hands
Are still beautiful, my consolation.
Years of silence has crept up
On both of us. Made a martyr

Out of me and a saint out
Of you. The big magic of solitude and loneliness
Has climbed into our souls.
You're as radiant as the sun.
The same sun that makes 'trees'
Out of all of us. After all this
Time you're still 'the one' to
Me but you're married now.
You've put down ancient and
Green roots in another city
That might as well be another
Country. The dream of you

Is still in my eyes. Life is hard
For me now and I wonder if you
Can understand that. That my
Silence is golden. My speech is silver
Like the centre of winter's flux.

The psychologist

There was a near death
Experience in the family.
We are at the game reserve.
Amongst mountain lions.
Blank strangers came.
They came with disorder.
Writing disorder.
Once spooked swans in a dream
I found myself on their lake.
Drowning in fields of black water.
Our eyes are made of fire.
She is the baby of the family.
Competition started at the swings.
Their lungs must be a mansion
covering the sharp milk estate of
the ghetto moon's craters.

All named after Jesuit priests.
To do lists, unfolding.
I am online. Repair.
That is where you will find me.
The magic of celebrity.
Of fame on earth planting itself there
Like Sherlock Holmes.
I drink in the lines of her face.
In the corners of her eyes.
Her mouth. I have lost her for good now.
Every season from childhood.
My spiteful humanity.
My shadow. I cannot catch

up to her. To our shared lessons
from our educationalist father
In the old fashioned wild.

Her bolognaise, lasagne, and paella

The English blood in the Khoi
Girl. The portrait of a young
Girl and handsome boy in
a giant sandpit. Both as hungry
as tigers, wolves, and lions.
My sister was my educationalist.
She refused to accept my myrrh.
My gold. Frankincense. My face of love.
The lines of her face shimmers with
glitter like the stars. Her genius is sexy.

Everyone, man, woman,
is in love with her.
She is a celestial being. Navigates
the world as an independent
Woman. She is a feminist.
A doer. A thinker. An intellectual.
She smells like a pineapple. Wood.
Who knows why we do what we do.
Once we used to dance
on the sea of grass of our
childhood. Once we were
puppets. Our doll mouths pulled open.

The world as humanity knows it
Miles away. Cracks showing in the system.
Coo. Coo. Cooing like babies.
Cooing like birds. Ostriches
With their heads in the sand.
This is a love song for a sister.

After all these years of feeling small
In her presence. It is Christmas
On the land. There is glitter
In her blood, on her skin, in her hair.
Life sails away from beyond
My reach at her kitchen table.

My fingers old roots

The divine strings of strategy.
Every year we had a new puppy.
Losing those animals does not matter
to me half as much as losing her.
A dense pain-body moved within me.
I imagined my parents
putting up house opposite
the hospital where I was born.
I imagine them moving furniture.
They guided my soul. She did too.
What she wants is a novel me.
What she wants is for me to grow up.
I am thirty-six and still left
out in the cold. Still living it "up" to her.
My rival's expectations.
You will never find her in
an encyclopedia. She will not
accept flowers. Tears for rain.
Rain for tears. Driftwood like the surgeon's
Gloves are temporary.

Goethe, Rilke, Tolstoy, Woolf

Alanis Morissette playing inside
my head. UFO in her eyes. A drum
made out of her mannequin limbs.
There is a desert in angelic
Poetry. I never forget these truths.
I am here on earth for a little
while where we flirt with the
Temptations of the world. Everything
is useless if it is not conquered
by love in the end. Humanity is
the unseen. The world is not my
Home. I have left the radiance of
the sunset and stars of childhood
far behind me. In my dreams I
return to the swings. The park, but now
it is all gold. On golden pond.
Gone are the passages. Goethe. Rilke.
Instead, what remains is the heart
of worship. Church. Hymns. Tithing.
Us, humanity desiring the same thing.
Long-term misery no longer making
Forward progress.

Xenophobia needs a psychiatrist

There's the mad dance of poverty on parade.
The haves and the have-nots.
The androgynous beauty of Virginia
Woolf's writing. Jean Rhys's depression.
Her alcoholism too. The poetry of Anne
Sexton, Keats, Rupert Brooke, S. Plath,
Ted Hughes with all of its quiet power.
Its iron, marrow and grit. I do not need
People half as much as I need the
Literature in my life. It has a sharp,
Incandescent beauty. Its radiance star-worship.
Literature the monster frightening
me the mouse. The monster beneath the bed.
I adore destroying myths. Stigmas.
The spoiled identity of the black child.

Desperate Slogans

We grew up in Swaziland.
Nature was our bridegroom.
Our fight song. And so I learnt to write about
Her parade-parade. The ego
Of rain that thinks she can wash
Away everything.
The windows to her soul. Her paradise.
Do fish know of distant planets?
The practical magic of the
Swimming pool is distant
To them but to me there is a conversation
In that milkshake, ice cream,
And enemy. I live now. Age later.

I was thirty-five when I read
a short story of Alice Munro's
In The New Yorker. I have
a cousin who lives there now.
She married an American.
She takes a bus into the city.
She has done what I have found
Impossible to do. Have children.
Be the Syria of cook and clean.
I do not make cauliflower bredie,
Eggplant curry, and tuna fish
Sandwiches. Eat pimento stuffed olives.
Instead I leave that to my mother.

Andre Brink

Her kids are American. In pictures
They draw in kindergarten
They have spaghetti meatballs
For heads. Her life is Americana.
She speaks with an accent.
On the phone in clipped American
Tones. Saying 'yeah' at the end
of her sentences. By now she
Probably believes in thanksgiving,
Turkey and reality television.
She does not read Bessie Head,
Joyce Carol Oates, Lauren Beukes.
Andre Brink. I don't think she's
Ever heard of Ingrid Jonker.
Perhaps my cousin did a poem of hers placed
In the curriculum in matric. That love affair
Inspired me. I wanted to
Write books like him.
Poems like Ingrid Jonker.

David wa Maahlamela

He came bearing gifts.
Of friendship and stories.
On his way to
The paradise of Grahamstown.
I have black notebooks.
Notebooks like any alchemist.
As black as crows.
In the late morning
I have enough typed pages to send
anywhere I want to. Mostly Europe,
the States, England, Africa.

Slaughterhouse cut

What do you do when there's
A revolution?
I remember sitting in my seat
At the South End Museum
In Nelson Mandela Bay
Next to my father listening to
A lecture. Thinking of George Botha.
I wished it would never
End like J.D. Salinger's
Classic 'Catcher in the Rye'.
The Manic Street Preachers sang
About Kevin Carter, yes, that
War photographer. I think
Of vultures as a metaphor. Thought
Of it as a slaughterhouse cut.

Stars above Cairo, Egypt

I see people all the
Time but they
Have become like an
Unmoving illusion.
Maidens, and men.
Women and children.
At night, I dream
Of Salinas, California.
John Steinbeck, and of
James Byron Dean.
My voice gone.
Leaf, tears, wind,
Voice, politics, flames.
Foundations of nature.
Gone, gone, and gone.
Every night I say farewell
To ghosts that go bump
In the middle of the night
In my childhood bedroom.
While traffic melts
Into the background.

For The Lovers Of Tea and Curcumin

It is an explosion –
This dream world
That is poetry and Alaska
My golden flesh
And the notebook
Of my spirit
The tenderness
Of the natural world
Madness is just
Another sickness
That will make
You tremble
That will make
You weep
Remember this

That there will never be
Anything extraordinary
About that
I don't need to love
Or be loved in return
As much as I need
To swim towards the light
Towards the illusion
That is both honesty and hostility
I find I must always be
Keeping the dog
On the leash as he discovers
The essences of humanity
Dirt and the altered states of mind

That keeps humanity under wraps

For poetry is another country
Far and away beautiful and lovely
A bride holding a book
The pages majestic and smelling
Of roses and together
We will discover
Why humanity
Is important to humanity?
Why is poetry needed?
By poets and humanity alike?
And what of the lovers of tea?
I will wrap the skin
And hair of Alaska
Around me like a shroud
And wear its veil and cover
With enthusiasm and pride.

For Lovers of coffee

Why skin and hair
The tapestry of flesh
I need trees and leaves
Grass and the seasons
Precious mountains and wild
Life with
All their simple
Orchestrated movements
The unmistaken frame
And rapture of it all
There's beauty
In everything
In the simple ceremony
Of pouring tea
Drinking it primitively

The sunrise is in
The image of a woman
Her femininity
What would we
Call that muscle?
Would we call those wings lungs?
A well of tidiness
Springing up relentlessly
There's blood in the old life
Blood in the new one
Prospering breath after breath
So empires are built
The crown of laughter

Poetry and studying
The poem's death

I winter amongst
Pale haunted icebergs
I winter amongst Sappho
Sup with plants and ghosts
Whatever
Is in the nature
Of praying meditatively
And of discovering
Happiness behind
The aloof façade
Of illness and sickness
Sickening creative ritual
And impulse is where
I live now – yonder
Where the glaciers are.

Leap of Faith

Finding myself
At the deep wreck
Of the world at large
He didn't need to tell
Me that all I had to do
To find him again and again
Was to read –
Read all the poetry
I could get my hands on
Sonnets and odes
It was as if I knew them
All off by heart
The silences within them
There's silence
All around me now

I've earned them those stripes
And the dead and the living
Go on and on like handsome tigers at the zoo
They are my companions
On this blue planet
From the beginning
Of pain, decay and growth
Until the end of days
And when it came to
Divorce and separation
All they knew of love
Was that they loved each
Other and it was enough
For both of them

In theory. Of pain they'd
Only learn of that later on
They would only remember
Their own childhood
When looking at the faces
Of love on the angelic shine
Of their children –
They'd whisper to themselves
Rapture, oh this must be it
Rapture! An atlas of it
Amongst all the difficulties
And how we've all drowned
In that lake with those cursed
Words calling themselves poetry.
Erosion

When I discovered
The person who I was
Supposed to love he
Was my fire to my flint
And in childhood
I danced
But also found myself quietly
Observing, studying
The minutia
This is where words
And language
Latin starts to bleed into belief
Serious brides. Serious women.
All of them cursed
All of them female poets
Was Eve really a lady?

Drifting from one world at large
To the next in search of material
Possessions to claim
As her own with her entourage.
There are ghosts
That bloom in this world
And there is nothing
That you can do about that
However intensely
Heaven might scar you
The spirit is so self-conscious
So self-pitying that it
Only speaks to us through
Our subconscious in valid ways
Silvery communion
Come to me please
Come to me – you are
Worshiping the wrong
God. You are in the
Presence of the wrong
Gods. Shroud cover me
Up completely. Take your
Veil and your tapestry too
Lift me towards the light
Towards glorious erosion
And what is left of the earth
Living in its ochre details
And so we dive into
The dream that is the sea.

Imaginary Oak

Wouldn't we all
If we could want to be
Threaded with the magnificence
Of love instead of the blurry
Reality of mourning
Clotting the blood
In our heart. Remembering
That love. I lost him beautifully
Wonderfully. In the ways
That men are supposed
To be lost. To other women.
To other children. His voice
Then became a rhyme.
Then it became an echo.
Mapping out difficulties

I did not conceive
Of anything except that I loved him
In ways that were not
Mutually exclusive.
I knew I had to have him
Not marry him
But the poetry in his eyes
Sparkled and his skin
Did as well and so I was
Caught up and my humanity reduced
Reflections
On the artist in me
That was dying

The madness was dying
But was also freeing

In unimaginative ways
I will live without him
By my side. Without his glare
Love will remain mysterious
Folded like origami beasts
People generally
Want to go all the way
When it comes to love
I'd rather stick to the straight
Path of impossible sadness

The Arctic Circle

She stood upon
That treasured wilderness
Praying about the
History that was sheltered
There. That stood tall.
And through her lips
Breathed the word, 'Arctic.'
This is desire.
The cleanliness, the purity
Of desire. With all
Its bedazzling rituals
That you covet or don't covet.
Jane Eyre was there.
And so was my mother
At twenty-five years old

The bride in her white lace.
Emily Dickinson was there.
Rapunzel and Eve too with their
Eyes and their hair like the sun.
This is what it is like
In the womb for girls
The days are pleasurable
There on that continent of ice
You taught me how to love
Even though it was forbidden
My fingers map out
The braveries of the atlas
Where men have tread before
Warriors – I desired you

Like hills desire valleys

The naming commodities
And being committed to them
My scars are budding
Blooming like flowers
And their vision is like an animal's
I find myself again
In the interiors of a room
The silence is a breakthrough
It is as cool as rain
I can feel a planting beginning
Through the tips of my fingers
Through this winter guest of mine
Over this threshold
There's a harvest farmers have
Committed themselves to.

Lover of Futility

All my life I have never wanted children
I have longed for companions but never children
To take care of or to take care of me
When I am at my most infirm in old age
I have always had a traveling heart
And that has been with me season after season
Of all the dark, mocking falling leaves.

There is stagnation between the laughter of clowns
That marks all of us. In the details of their heavy made-up
Faces. The wigs that hides their true features from all of us.
There is a sadness and a pathetic frustration
That lies there like the trees at the bottom of a lake.
Drowning visitors every one never to be seen
By humanity again. Touched by the hands of humanity
Again. And so we say that our fears have lethal airs
And graces. We begin to search for the exit out.
Our moral compass navigates us through the elements
Of air and fire. And whenever our hearts are pure again

We the lovers of futility and imposters
In our dreams. We will become voyagers once again
Our minds and hearts turned into ice, asylum pieces
Every one. The frame psychological. The work
The world and the fabric of the universe darker still
Than our childhood. A child's world touched by
Swaziland's mountains, valleys, Lazarus and greener
Pastures, sleep and the richness of a father's madness.
Humanity goes forward into the exploratory studies
Of both man and woman to find souls there

Some find that they are touched by love

Others find mental sickness, and aberrations
Illness composed of jagged pharmaceuticals, doctors
And pharmacists, a bright palace of harmonious
Music, lords and ladies of the stellar night
Dancing their cold hearts and lungs out as fast
As their legs and feet can carry them. They don't
Need a world of inquiries. They're all strangers
In the dead of night and they're all singing the blues.
Stringing, threading, braiding love knots, Scout
Knots, clotting blood knots feeling the tightness
In their chests while the rest of us live and die.

Lover of Jane Eyre

Come with me to this wide open place
This place of husband and wife, companions
This known yet unknown place of wonder
There is still a distance from the rest
Of the planets, the turning moon and sun
The tides of the ocean, the Pacific and Indian
Which is where we'll keep on meeting
When there is a scarcity of the faces of love
Reach deep within yourself and look inside your heart
For all the assumptions that are lying there
In wait for you drenched in circumspection
For child are you not a warrior made in perfection?
The laws of suffering are not meant for you
It is not the place for you. Your childhood
Filled you with dignity and hope will not empower
You but also uplift you. You with your mind
Are meant for a beautiful life filled with passion
And many dappled things such as the poetry
Of language of the wreck at the end of the world
The gracious lady that is the ship wreck and light house
Waves may have called to you like they did to that ship
For you are not just imagined. You are a myriad of things.

Lover of Prairies

I know what I have to be delivered from
It is silence, the despair of silence, the bleak
Landscape of the rural post-apartheid countryside
But I need the fragrant air that is vital, fresh
My bones need to acquire it – that certain pleasure
My lungs need to be filled with more than grace
I am in need of wings and a rosary
You are reduced to be being a thing that is worshiped
Put on a pedestal or put on a throne wearing a crown
Once you were that sought after
You were the vision that we have of ourselves
Enough to transform and transfigure our souls
Winters will be deposited here long after
We have summered here in the hot zone of this climate
You are the filthy lover of this dream I have of you
You are the dreamer and the exotic perfumed one
You are my cure for me to be purified and my tonic
How I long for your arms and for your warm embrace
You are my extraordinary emergency service
Bright, vivid, vivacious and signalling red
War is my country but then again so are you
My Paris, my Hemingway, my moveable feast.

Lover of the Chandelier

They spoke of wealth (of course I had none)
Their clothes spoke of it, their speech and their
Blonde-honeyed hair, every freckle on their nose,
Knee and cheek. It was always flowers
And poetry that made my broken heart smile.
The light from the sun. Now that was my chandelier.
I always wonder why I felt so small in your world
You are still my dream as tender as a Paris meadow
Diving into the closet under the bed
Filled with monsters and with wild beasts
Dressed to the nines dressed to impressed
I am that woman who sleeps alone who eats alone
In her forest. I wait and watch for you the flowing river
In childhood we were loyal to each other
We were blossoming us sisters and that is the truth
You were my manna from heaven
You were my Moses and my burning bush
I believed that you existed with all your airs and graces
You took your powerful singing place amongst
All the gods and goddesses and I worshiped
You then as I worship you then as you dance
Far and away outwards from my embrace.

The Winter Branches

This daughter has grit
And brick walls and all
A solitary moon
In all her feverish anticipation
Waiting upon the machine
And those ancestors.
Why do I suffer in relationships?
There's a darkness within me
There's a darkness within you
I don't take kindly to your jokes
Nor the endless possibility
In your voice and the masterpiece
That is your world
Your splintered home
At the end of the world

These winter branches are mine
The anniversary of this winter
Is also mine. My mute grief
Over every black leaf is mine
I need to see you in a photograph
I need to see you painted
In oils and watercolours
There's the existence of faith
And pure hope as I take you in my arms
To have and to hold
From this day forward
Jubilant is the trumpet and saxophone
All their rituals have logic
I stand mute at the edge of the lake

The lake's mouth
Is full of jeweled water
Wind drifts like driftwood
The weight of water is inescapable
What is human? This stain
Is human. What is beautiful?
Eyes and this ordinary madness.
What captures the light?
Klimt. Is it injustice? Sickness?
The right and the wronged?
There's too much earth and world
In the desire that we have for each other
We have captured our lungs for eternity
This landscape was fashioned by a gardener
This letter is meant out of love.

Lover of Children

No daughters and sons have I although
I am still a lover of other mothers' children.
I delight in them. I have discovered I can
Do clever things with my hands. Artistic things.
Instead of braiding hair I can intuitively thread words.
They are my fish. It is no longer winter here.
I am no longer a guest in my own country
I praise your silence and the personal space
You left behind and I feel the tightness in my heart
I praise you I praise all of you but most of all
I have been left behind in a tunnel into the black
There is insomnia even in a sermon
And electric wavelengths in a lecture room
A female writer journaling away in her diary
But where are the children and the husband
She has none. She is afraid of those words
That those words will make cell walls around her
That those words will become her prison
Winter with its shark teeth that threatens
To overwhelm her every waking thought and moment
She thinks of grief and remembers her childhood
And the fact that her mother never held her hand

When she crossed the road or believed in her
When looking left then right what is she grieving for?
What is she living for? What is she praying for?
Midnight's children. Children who live under the bridge
They smoke cigarettes as if their lives depended on it

In another poem. In another lifetime, another life
There was a mistake. There was a little obsession
A predestined promise of procrastination that smelled
Like perfume. And then too soon you will realise
That you should not have walked away in that moment
Even though you were forgiven child of God
Child of an extraordinary God stripped of all
Illusion and fear of expectation
And like Marie Antoinette was led to a guillotine
Aren't we all at some stage in our lives?
Don't we have to live with our misgivings?
And with being misrepresented, dancing around
Golden laughter in our mouths that we don't
Want to escape from. We want to search forever more
For that most singular delusion swinging swiftly
I like my innocence and I like my imperfections
I like the fact that I'm flawed and that I'm confessing to it.

There is nothing lost in translation when coming home to the mock husband

I am not coping because I am not the doctor. Because I am not the one who is fluent in the doctor's language no matter how hard I try. How will I be able to benefit from wearing that white laboratory coat, stethoscope around the neck, with that particular bedside manner? Where is my infinite piano? Watch this. Watch this romance. It is clever math, no, it is elegant math with all of its violent alertness under my fingertips. What is the weather like in Los Angeles? What is a winter like in Los Angeles? What will my head say to my heart as I walk on that beach, or breathe in that valid air from that Parisian meadow with my moral compass to navigate me on those open roads, the wide open spaces of the Midwest? What will my limbs say to each other in London if I ever get around to having that London experience forgoing all my responsibilities as a writer and a poet in South Africa? For isn't that what I am first and foremost. A South African writer and poet living in a post-apartheid apocalyptic city. City life as opposed to life in the rural countryside. Searching for greener pastures in the asphalt garden where everything is golden and chameleon-like. I have never wanted the experience of loss. The measure of loss but life has given me that responsibility. Sutures too.

And panic and I have had to thread both against threadbare knuckles. I have covered myself up with an American quilt. It has become my shroud. It has become my cover in other poetry. But I feel it all the time now. The warmth of anxiety. I feel it humming, humming, and humming in my bones. Singing to the leaves on the winter trees. Guests every one. They're like bees. They're a rapturous swarm. What do I know without having a sophisticated culture, a knowledge and education beyond this tidal moon and sun and then I think of the planets. How like the planets I am? I know my place. I know my place so well now that I cannot give it up. And why would I? There will never be a case of mistaken identity. All I will ever know about life is the predictions of Sappho, poetry and writing. And how sometimes how beautifully unpredictable life can be otherwise. There are storms in the dark and we need to speak about the acute pain from those storms in beautiful and wonderful ways. Mostly the image of depression is that of a wild thing. When I'm crazy I know that is when I am most alive. When I am not crazy, when I am most sober is also when I am most alive but I don't know it. All feeling leaves me and I long for the stress of crazy. I long for someone to tell me I'm beautiful.

You are mine. The pain of Sarajevo is in my blood. Mingled there in my blood. Staring back at me in my blood and but what can I do but stare back at it? The door was somehow left ajar for me and my heart was bursting. It ready to be split open like a pomegranate. Seeds everywhere like seawater. I found wild oblivion, the safe passage from suffering in those seeds. At first I could not speak of the fantasy that I held in my hands and that my head wished for so ardently. I could not interpret those promised lands that my mocking husband returned from. I needed land and yet I needed to be reborn as well. I needed stress, a tour of the flesh like I needed the back of my hand. I flickered and then I was buried once again amongst the flowers. And with dirt upon my head I soon realised that I was supposed to be the beautiful keeper of the vanished and the unexamined. The apprehended. I do not want to age. To age means to give up your mortality like an artist giving up their brushes. To age means to give up everything. To age means that you are not bold

84

anymore and that you don't have anything to be brave over. It just happens to be in your blood to think these things. Never mind how you try not to. I need to write to you of the quiet courage of our mothers and our grandmothers. So pay attention.

Birthday Notes

Grief is only a warning. Denial too.
I need to find out why the brightness dies
And the flowers heads. Every one.

Brazil

Women are made
of scraggy landscapes.
Thirst. Stormy nights.
Their limbs are old-fashioned.
Antiques. Paradise.
They are always reminding
me of Ezra Pound's
Alba wherever I go.

Their pastures
are made of Paulo's veins.
Remote-controlled.
Gold flows in those veins.
Women love their
collections of crockery.
These lovers of tea.
Of poetry. Every tear

is a symphony in their eyes
are sparks of fireworks.
A projection surface.
Their tears are sap.
Their blood the colour
of quartz.
They move in villas
as if life was a tragedy.

Women made of
short hair and razors.
They go along a waterfall's

pilgrimage. Creep into
the lion's den.
They know this banquet
is only made for one now.
Even earth has scars.

If it were a wedding,
it would be a different
story. It would be a different
kind of poem. Poetry.
Have a different
ending. Beginning
with a setting in a church.
Ending with a childbirth.

Nadine Gordimer

Infirm in old age –
Of dark, mocking falling leaves.
A Kafkaesque quiet.

Laws of attraction –
The pain body of summer.
Black hair is my fish.

Another country –
Whales. Poetic explosions.
Tapestries of flesh.

Pomegranate tree –
I am wet through. My arms rain.
Code written in braille.

Lost in translation –
Never tell the whole story.
Worship the body.

Thanks for the water fat –
The wreck is tangled in leaves –
Spells smashes the glass.

Moth and butterfly –
We will go to the black grave.
With your cursed language.

Metamorphosis –
Letters of hope. Suffering.

From that hot climate.

All things Orlando –
Bodies found in the wetlands.
Women disappeared.

Fed on coconut –
Women must keep diaries.
The bedroom is cold.

Endangered species –
Joy fills my lungs with ice wolves.
The milk flowers. A-white-mess.

Psychosis. Sadness –
There are two kinds of decay.
Echoes too have routes.

NoViolet Bulawayo

Rag doll –
This is the scene. In your orbit.
I am your sun.

We pick up sticks –
The ball of the moon glitters.
In the dead of night.

In childhood –
Everything has a tongue.
I want to be called Alice.

My name is not Alice –
The ghost of apron strings.
I want a Cheshire cat.

Mummy's roast –
Sunday afternoons everlasting.
The chicken wears a shroud.

Death to the bully –
Children fall in love with twins.
Childhood light is honest.

The lonely child –
Let literature move them.
Let nature find them.

Wind in their hair –
Its fractured bulb planting itself

Like a cornucopia.

Skinny legs –
A glass of milk. Buttered bread.
Shadows are pillars.

Counting the hours –
Throat married to tongue.
Tongue to landscape.

When someone knocks –
The child will look out of the window.
Chattering like a ghost.

Under the bedspread –
There is an extinct volcano.
A castle. Thrones. Horses.

Nancy Sinatra

Driftwood –
There is a worm in my lovesick soul.
That is eating its way through.

Yet my heart is formidable –
I am left breathing in the morning air.
Beautiful like a rare piece of glass.

Grabs her umbrella –
She leaves without saying goodbye.
Cape Town's Table Mountain sighs.

Confetti. She is one of them –
Stars shine through cosmic surfaces.
I pull them down like fabric.

You meet a man –
You fall in love. This is what happens.
To daughters.

When you are a woman –
It becomes you to be a wife, a mother.
If he leaves you. You feel betrayed.

You do not tell her this –
It would mean the death of her.
The likely death of you.

Snowdrop –
The bees have no wrinkles.

All I want is my smokes.

My cigarettes –
I remain neutral to the pitiable.
Latecomers in the dark.

Loaf –
Concentration is a game.
I must eat like a prophet.

Her lips are too red –
Let her figure this out for herself.
Tulips have gone retrograde.

Porcelain figurine –
Statuesque at a wedding.
Cactus lost in a desert.

What I have in common with the paper tiger empress from Smith

Desire, grief and loneliness were rivals –
I think of the memoirs that I have written
Of excursions, of executions, of experiments.
How I mourned.

I mourned the nothing loss of him –
Like spies. Smoke. Fat of the land. Mirrors.
In my moonlight house. The forests
Are armed.

It was difficult. I saw him in things –
Exits. Then not at all. It took me a long time
To triumph over all things. In the end I saw
Heaven.

All lightning is a lake of silver –
Tonight there is only a portal to Hades.
I needed sunlight. It was a golden ticket.
Like any prayer.

I endure summer nights. I endure sorrow –
Endure her invited guests at the banquet.
The uninvited well I imagine their deaths.
Like childhood.

It is dark here. I am trying too hard –
There is a great fire within me like a sea.
No flowers grow here. No grassiness.

No books.

Burial lies behind the closed door –
Closure. The villagers are waiting in the barn.
I am not giving up my psyche's souvenirs.
Gretel dances.

I tasted the syrup of the perfect ending –
Cold, malignant fish I do not accept you.
The assignment is a game of win and lose.
Lectures are given.

Give me the contents of romanticism –
The white rabbits are ruling the wonderland.
Memory is clouded. Images paralyse me.
The lamp is bright.

Elijah's Five Haiku

A winter story –
Even the fog is on edge.
The hanging woman.

You are a memoir –
A room filled with black silence.
Blue and black sleeper.

Here is your poem. Birch –
The moonlight crosses water.
These are my last words.

Red is my colour –
The event was the rival.
The balloons are kind.

Flower mannequin –
This is my parliament's face.
A ghost is calling.

Charles Bukowski

Eyes closed. Goals realized.
Well, at least this day's goals.
I feel a dampness on my cheek.
Rain. I watch the ducks.
I watch the children feeding the ducks.
Thinking of the slow train
Of searching. Of hours.
Of infatuation. Of clever love
That smells like Paris, France.
What is this cathartic punishment?
Loneliness. Solitude. Futility.
I choose myself. Nothing else.
Nobody else. Not the bottle of gin.
Not a cigarette. Foot traffic.
This terrifying din. Citizens.
We are all case studies. Histories.

Are you my nemesis, sin?
Some people are independent.
Some are modern. Some are bold.
Somebody else a wife, mother,
Lover missing their personal freedom.
Then there are the suicides.
Missing persons on television screens.
How quickly love turns to hate.
The heart growing bitter. Cold.
God sometimes he ceases at once.
It is winter in the city. Nothing
Can be more beautiful than
Seeing how the afternoon light hits

The page. It inspires a relationship
With the divine. A man and
A woman in love. Children.

Jane Campion

This is my story. My atlas.
My Kingdom Come.
It first began in high school for me.
In that dysfunctional suffering
Of our house. The supposed sanctuary.
You were the brave, spirited –one.
As brown as a berry. Healthy.
Inside my head were long letters.
Winter in your hair. In your hands.
The ingredient list for bolognaise.
This is what you do so well.
I do not know what made you brave.
A success.

Perhaps it is because you never
Wrote me about America,
India, Phuket, Thailand.
You came home with a suitcase
Filled with a Christmas-addict's gifts.
The silence in my bedroom.
The silence in the rooms
Of our childhood house. Bipolar.
Inside my head were green apples.
Those long, boring letters that
You never read. I was not brave
Enough to post them. You never
Complained.

I have a theme song for everything.
Avocado season. Summer.

A feast of olive flesh on the tongue.
Poetry. A museum of avocados.
You never cried. I cried about everything.
Pan's ticking crocodile
Is on your left shoulder.
I cried for everything that was lost.
The fat ghost of our love
Has a long way to go
Tinkerbell sits on your
Right shoulder. Your adult voice
Of reason. A baptism.

Virginia Woolf

I am free as a soldier
With children underfoot.
Understanding the measure
Of loss in these times
It is not an easy thing to do
It observes calculations.
Solutions. My love comes from
My heart. My soul. There is a
New footprint now for this
Continent. Country after
Country. Those ravaged, those
War-torn, those newborn
Democracies complete with
Female president. Those with
The refugee camps. I go to church.
Do you feel the same? All loved up.
On the other hand, sad. Mournful.
Knocking on wood.

I trace my fingers over
A lover's initials. Of course, I understand
It is over. I am not free anymore.
I watch leaves fall.
Feel the wind floating on air.
In once upon a time generations
From now cinematography
Will exist as well as an editor.
Focus groups. They will sing
The praises of an artist
Simply known as Basquiat or

102

Artists known as Any Warhol
Perhaps I would have been a fan.
A fan of cinema, Dorian Grey.
Of Jackson Pollack. They have
Not invented the delete key.
See traces of the kingdom of God
In the clouds. I rub my fingertips
Against the rough bark.
Gazing up at the blue dissolve.
I try to convince myself I made
The right decision. After all,
I am still free in other ways.
Defined ways. Infinite ways.

Sea Creatures

(a poem in experimental haiku)

Milk is a vision –
Barefoot sewed to the shoreline.
Gulls are sweet as dew.

Driftwood plucked from air.
You are a lifetime ago.
Ghost story – sea.

Mapping stems – flora
What resides there is a glove.
Echoes. Avocados.

The science of winter –
Champagne's protein flourishes.
Even pigs eat fruit.

The mouth is too smart –
The warmth of the soloist.
Leaves fall to the ground.

Precious childhood games –
Bleak winter groans. Holding hands.
Small sea creature. Ghost.

Kind of royalty –
My dad is a piano.
Pomegranate seed.

Doors open. Frozen –
The sun breathes like a furnace.
Pumping in and out.

Too pretty. Too thin –
Forests are educated.
Yes, significant.

Elixir of life –
The posed fruit of living cells.
Prose. Food for thought.

Young lover's suicide –
Romeo where art thou hatched?
She has sprung the ark.

Elijah said so –
Because Elijah said so.
Novels remind us.

Poems, Excitable Pursuit and the Company of Words
(For Sylvia Plath)

Tonight I want to eat pasta and forget the collective past
Exploding into superior life yet quite alone at the end of the
world
When God made awesome you I could stand silence
You of all people will be sorely missed like milk and bread
And poppies whose beauty is screaming to be heard
The day I found you I was struck by the weather
And I listened to the evening rain as it poured into my soul
Locked into its own wintry ego it tasted like waiting ice cream
The grandeur of London and a single woman flying solo

Damaged is the state of the weight of bittersweet rain
The diary that fell from the sky and every day my promise is
To dig a little deeper for her, to find her in the crush of
Keepsake data, empress of mine did I always have weight
issues?
There was a summing up of limbs in childhood continued
Where the indifferent chicken says, 'Please eat me.'
The pudding is a Smiler and it has my heart – it is smiling at me
And I wish I could stop worshiping the potatoes so
I do remember how angelic the table looked piled with feast

Mummy is my angelic link bound for paradise and from
The moonlight in her hair and her vowels she knitted me
together
In her womb as fast as she could crochet cells and nucleic acid
together
I am looking at my reflection, studying it and it feels as
If I have already spent a lifetime here in this world and then

There's you but I must forget you, push off towards tomorrow
Oats and then the sky is more than company
Because it is where I meet my destiny, my nation –
Personas standing in a Zen-line of succession

I know that nothing can purify me now – not anything
Poised and anchored achievement will not make up lost time
Where there lies a fragile reckoning of an inheritance
Of earthly ritual between mother and daughter
I look at all of my achievements and how it wasn't enough
It wasn't enough to save me from the fact Mum didn't love me
In front of me lies Athol Fugard's road and my 'first piece of
stature'
To come out of earthy ritual, soil – an achievement
I confess then I will be safe, wise and once more have courage.

The Climate in the Northern Areas

The actor with their deceptive perspective
The offering from the salt of the earth burnt by the sun
Angelic link between the owl and the moon
And the aware moon is a beloved and ancient witness
To the stars, to evil, to the human race
And all their purification rituals and dreams
Dreams between mother and daughter
Son and father, adopted prize, paper fragment
The lines of all these things appear in a hopeful climate
The lines are there complete. I am still chemistry.
Particles lingering and floating in the air – romantics everyone
They came from all over (my observations).
Observations from childhood at a glance
I am only the passionate instrument of my faith
Warrior of light it is almost heaven
Wounded as my soul is wounded is not every soul?
There is an authentic contract drawn up
Between earth, the universe and humanity
Poverty will be the death of all of us.
I was mum's second choice – I had no inheritance
Men drink women in for hours on this side of town
Children no longer live in an age of innocence
Each one suspicious, rough, picking up bad habits.

After the birds flew away winter came
This is what I can see with 'my eyes' – tasting the bread of life
I waited all winter for the heat of summertime
There was silence in every room of the house
A fire in my heart that burned as bright
As a moth's pilgrimage towards the light

There was a common sense of the world inside my head
I walk into the sea and feel the weight of water
Against my spirit and my body – the sky is a wild blue
So here I am now there I was then I don't know
How it came about the writing part of me that bit
Those goals I never thought I'd become a poet
The waves broke over my head drowning visitors everyone
The silver lining makes every being a living survivor
Navigating from this world to the next
Even the strained mother-daughter relationship
Will fill the fridge with thanksgiving food
It hurts when I smile at strangers
It feels as if I am drowning in a waterfall
And now we come to unconscious love and passion
Your first hurt, your first love, your first everything.

And Four Women

And Alice's oyster shell

Where has everyone gone?
Into the trippy harsh climate of hedonistic and decadent
nostalgia
They've preferred it over and above life, existence, sitting in a
room
Filled with the knife edge of silence, the sharp depth of it,
reading
Literature from that Austrian great Rilke, people have appeared
To prefer the empire of the sun to the cold, preferred sacrifice
and conversation
I hate the word suffer. Sacrifice. Surreal but there's a brightness
to sensitivity
Vulnerability, imagination, visionaries (was Alice a visionary)
and understanding.

Etty Hillesum's world of wonderland

The house is so quiet (where has everyone gone?)
I have found a book am reading fragments from a diary
It contains love letters, a German love story, and a story about
a concentration camp
She is feeding my brain in all those vulnerable spaces with all
This bedazzling information (the diary belongs to a Dutch Jew
Who was captured near the end of the war)
She was captured near the end of the war and I wondered
Did she ever miss flowers when she was in that camp?

Was Alice a mystery?

Was Alice a visionary sitting down to tea parties in a
wonderland?
And following a white rabbit? Was she a girl with the soul
consciousness
Of a Brahmin? It feels as if every day I've died a little
Dug a little deeper to the roots of a granadilla Southern Africa
To find my sister like a keepsake, my empress from my
childhood
With this little heart of mine I feel I will no longer continue to
shine
If I do not have her autumn love, her discontentment is my
discontentment.
Big, bright neon lights burning in a city filled with bold people,
old people
Young people, star people, couples, families, homosexuals
Buying art and property in a Johannesburg that has stopped
calling me
Why will not she believe me? Instead I can be found cooking
with layers
I left people behind in my past behind glass walls, brick walls
They've all evaporated from my sight, these lessons, and those
songs
The man that I loved I have lost him forever to his wife and his
children
Wasted years but not a waste of my intuition, not a waste of
intimacy
She tells me that she is going to London at the end of the year

Then I take a breath

The second sex comes of age when a man wounds them
like an animal or washes away their childhood sins, or whispers

in their ear
Sweet nothings and tells them that they have lovely bones.
We are not normal unless loved. Until we are tangled in the
obsession of it.
Will you catch me if I fall?

The Ballad of the Near-Wasted Generation

As I progress towards you, towards possession
Lost in Jane Austen, Emily Dickinson, wuthering heights,
America
English literature, Rilke's letters to a young poet
I draw lines through the clouds in the air picturing every
Silver lining that passes me by
Through God's flute comes a prayer like a jewel in the dust
The unbearable bittersweet lightness of youth,
And being young at heart and torn, I'm dreaming all at the
same time
There's a river that runs through it, a legend of a river, epic
Like the feeling that you have when you're in love with a film
star
There's always an open road ahead, a mirror to my soul.

South Africa, South Africa, South Africa, South Africa
Do you remember the forced removals, apartheid, and
swimming
In a river, when there was a department for Colored Affairs?
There was no white bread toasted for your breakfast, no jam,
No boiled egg, red cappuccino, daddy and mummy reading the
morning newspaper
You garden boy, you kitchen girl were treated like lepers, worse
than dogs
You were raped, cheated and bullied, butchered and murdered,
Suburbs were pillaged and turned into slums overnight and a
sharp light
Drifted into focus. Some days would have a brave sweetness
about it
Other days the near-wasted generation would venture out to

kill or be killed.
Slow men, slower women, and mute children.

Africa, Africa, Africa, and Africa once again I am devoted to
you
What does love feel like for you. The link to the international
outside world
I want to be saturated by you. I have seen glimpses of your
trauma.
Your suffering, the genocide, civil war, unrest, refugees, camps,
the slave trade
I've seen glimpses of the colour of your children's skin.
Albino, white, colored, black, mixed race, and everyone is as
precious as porcelain
Under our sky even the soft and hard Lolita, the promiscuous,
the prostitute,
Young men with that arrogant filter from their heads to their
mouths
Our gathering of musicians and poets are like the circle of the
golden sun
I don't care for the ego, for these things anymore – the
paraphernalia of violence
And for the discontent for so many is a permanent assignment
for them.

As I progress towards you, towards possession
With an almost criminal intent, carrion and Kevin Carter on my
mind
Moses Molelekwa, Dulcie September, George Botha, Brutus
and Biko,
Including Lumumba this is my story, suffering in silence is not
unique

Making it is making it through to the other side, perhaps this is why
Communities are afraid of speaking about it – soloists everyone
Some say there is such a violent intent on this planet to destroy, to sabotage
But there are still ways of finding peace, of finding yourself amidst sanctuary
Inviting people to your sanctuary is out of the question
Everyone must journey and find their feet on their own pilgrimage
I am still revisiting the past, still rewriting history and I guess I always will.

Rwandan Ephemera

It was the year of literature for me. It was the year of picking out books
that would make me feel glorious and unique for being a female writing in an
age of iron, still dominated by males. It was the year of missing people from
childhood, from high school, an aunt who was so far away from me who died
from cancer, another family member who I regarded as my second mother who
passed on after a short illness. It was the year I first spoke those words.
She did not have to go, I said. Her death was untimely, I said. These days I
am catching up on my reading. Reading all those books I should have read in
high school and university. I am reading The Waves by Virginia Woolf. Have
yet to finish Mrs. Dalloway. Have yet to start on The Voyage Out and her
essays and lectures. Am feeling gloriously in tune with stream of
consciousness writing. Am positively glowing with it. I write best in that
niche but was told to explore other avenues as well. The year is ending but
a writer and a poet's work is never done. I am more tired in the evenings

now. The more I think of the 'ballad of Sylvia and Ted', the more I think of

the ballad of my own parents, of my own failing health problems. How they do

not fit anymore into that otherworldly wheel of perfectly matched

individuals who get married fit into. How my father is not a repair type of

person or a repairperson. I think of waves. Woolf's waves. From childhood to

growing, becoming more and more set in your ways, becoming elderly. I think

of the waves breaking against Sylvia Plath's shore. My Hiroshima. The

Hiroshima of my parents' own making. When you write you have to get used to

the solitude. It almost pains me to say this. You take all your wounds, all

your walking woundedness, all your scar tissue, all your shouty emotions and

you spread it all out in front of you and then you begin to put everything

in mental boxes. Arrange out of them and label them all with 'Pandora'. Only if you feel like it. Remember, these are also treasures

so treasure them. Treasure your thoughts because they are precious.

As precious as ephemera, the miracles of glaciers and Rwandan butterflies.

The Clock is an Animal

Letting go of the (earth I cupped in my hands)
was like the letting go of a small piece of fabric.
Eating birthday cake. The edge of a tapestry.
In the understanding of the surrendering
I could feel it. I could feel winter or at least there was
wintering in those long hours. Those hospital hours.
There it was indefinitely and then it was inside of me.
Draining away and then some. Clattering like rain on the roof.
A flood of pigeons on the roof. I waited for midnight. I knew
then
I would fall asleep. Dream of the feast of hills and mountains
of Swaziland. Never forgetting the mousetrap
Between the kitchen floor and me.
Futility pains me, it kills me to say this.

It is as if the wound (that stain) has come into contact
with the air. As if, the blood ripens somehow on contact.
I think of the trains of my childhood. Taking me far away from
The planet of my birth, Port Elizabeth to Johannesburg.
(My mother's people. Johannesburg's people).
From the flat opposite the library. Now I eat paella.
Drink red cappuccino. Make a performance out of it.
My brother and sister are old enough to drink wine.
They drink too much of it. The Middle Ages has caught up
with me.
The beach I remember from childhood is gone.
The mother I remember from childhood is gone.

All I remember is studying the Bible fastidiously.
Writing has become like an infection. I pour religion

Into it and indoctrinate people on essays, prose, haiku,
But my favourite is poetry. People worship what
They do not understand. They call it genius or they
Either call you mad. The poet waits a lifetime
For them to come around to him or her. In other words,
They must surrender the noose around their neck
Some time. Others concentrate on licking the spoon
From a childhood of licking spoons. Are you also
Afraid to be alone with your childhood fears.
Please unearth those monsters with foreign beaks.
You will find order and classes amongst the wretchedness
And the wretched of society. You will find both
The orchestral living there and lost property coming up for air

Shura

My flesh, my blood and your stem ill and bitter
Sink deep into your grave my little bold skinned flower
So small with your weak limbs heiress in your mother's arms
You killed an angel you filthy exotic paranoid foreigner
With your orange silks, bangles at your wrists.
Known beloved, known neurotic will you ever be forgiven?
In death both of you will thrive at Ted Hughes's bone-clinic
And you will whisper that war your majesty is a crime.
My dreamer, love poem, sonnet and my shell, my hell.
Death is a monster, a shell, while the sea is a ghost.
The air is beautiful, is it not like a Parisian soul?

The combinations of water in a glass, the clarity of words,
A white meringue of a beautiful dress, is it mine, is it mine?
My stories are fragmentary; my poetry is terrible because
I say it is so it is so. My love for you is a blank thrill.
It is dying. Shame. But I have brought it upon myself you see.
I dislike my conversation. I have drilled it into myself. Gas.
This emptiness. Talent is my enemy. I wish to cry. You have
left.
Regard me no more as lover. I will take the promises you made
to the grave. You will stand at the mouth of it, its purse.
Together Shura and I will rest in eternity. I will cling to her.
I do not need your soul. Our spirits are clouds, numb, celestial.

Everything, the earth is diminishing in front of my eyes.
People have become puppets. Winter has power over my
mood.
There is no man on the moon. He has disappeared for good.
The angels have seen to that. Only a feminist remains. She is

fair.

She is my gift to you, to Shura. No more harm will come to us now.

My mouth is frozen. My lips are blue with cold. My limbs, my limbs.

I cannot feel them. You chiseled them out of thin air of ghosts. I am distancing myself more and more away from you. Evaporate.

Your father is responsible for this. I am off the edge. Leaning Towards bleeding intelligently, rain is a feast and so is morals. But you knew nothing of the latter brute, beast, traitor, and coward.

It hurts that you hurt me and that you hurt Shura too.

But what is pain my lotus flower? But sacrifices have to be made.

Why always the vulnerable, the wounded, the sick and troubled?

My beauty was accidental until glaciers came between us.

I wish I had destroyed you now, not romanced, and not seduced you.

Now I only have the capacity within me for spring, to swim.

Tel Aviv and Canada both distant memories I trained myself to grow wise.

The night is different now. I feel it all the time. Shura in my arms.

We are both prisoners. I can never make plans. She will never grow old.

Ted Hughes's ugly duckling will never grow into a swan.

She, my Shura will never fall in love and whose fault is that.

Reading Cook Books On The Sly

I've found the abandoned
Collected everyone I've come upon
Some have been scattered far and wide
Fast beneath the wards of hell
Some have been found useful
In their being, in their humanity
They have found their place on my canvas

Visitors have come to look at my canvas
Near future ghosts unnamed and unarmed
Hiding behind clean columns like Samson
The All-out-for-Revenge quilt covers sinners like me
Magda and the quiet society she kept
It came out of my head
When a poet dies there are always notes on grief

It is not something I want to take on
The secret life of all the connections
The abstract metaphor in every one
Like an exhibit on show for the world to see
Even the mannequins and the swans' society
He has to deal with the pain somehow
He has to control it and his sadness too

Sons and daughters they've raised
Cloth of love they've shared for years
Cancer attacked the foundation – took them off
To hell for a decade and a half (called off remission)
I left them alone to catch a thief killing time
It's hellish isolation, to have a broken wing
To wait for healing, the therapy in recovery

Cancer reached the wuthering heights of America
It became a country at war with itself
Child soldiers marching through – matchstick men everyone
Thinking that they were the nation's best
I didn't place fresh dirt or wilted flowers on her grave
Water the wreathe, put a name to every face
That was there on that day

That made me feel so small and inadequate
We weren't intimate friends but did that matter
In the end nothing did because with time
You forget and there is a kind of peace
In the forgetting that way – something is healed
Something is healed completely
This is the price I have paid and I must live with it.

Ethan

Cherub, you're a constellation prospering
Your voice is lyrical, magic, and full of depth
Always rise again angelic little one
The world around you is waiting upon your arrival
Star people sit with their notebooks. Suns navigate them
They all have routes that border on God to follow
Under the blue steel of the sky's history wilderness

Learn how to dance, collect shells and driftwood wrapped
Around seaweed on the beach, catch the ball,
Have a wandering soul in all of your dreams, and always
journey
Moving forward, follow your guardian angel's instinct
Remember Biko, and that difficult thoughts come from the
heart
Think of silence when you experience deep pain
It is only a season. It will pass. Continue to journey moving
forward.

Are the trees not beautiful? Climb them. Build a tree house.
Play pretend. Pretend you are lost in a forest. You will find
God and silence, loss and suffering there.
And when you grow up you will unfortunately realize
That mankind is a violent species capable of brutality.
Childhood, innocence and purity is a gift bestowed upon us.
Live in that world and for as long as possible taste its
sweetness.

You are so beautiful, so loved but one day
You will come to know of evil, great evil
It isn't anybody's fault really it is just the way
The world looks like on a canvas, how its machine turns and
works
It is another language, light can't be found there
But for now the world you live in is perfectly lovely
You're surrounded by dream keepers

The wind touches your head outside in the garden.
You reach out for it with your arms; kick out with your legs.
You want to steal it with your wizened fingers.
And the world is clean, your family is a vision
There is nothing about a punishment of it.
Your mother holds you. Your father looks on proudly.
You are his son, his son, his son. He smiles

And it almost breaks my heart
But why should hearts be breaking?
Next month you will be a month old.
You are growing nicely.
You are as strong as a tiger (everybody loves you).
Every day you are showered with kisses
It must come from all that love that we have stored up since
childhood.

Mmap New African Poets Series

If you have enjoyed *Young Galaxies*, consider these other fine books in the **New African Poets Series** from *Mwanaka Media and Publishing*:

I Threw a Star in a Wine Glass by Fethi Sassi
Best New African Poets 2017 Anthology by Tendai R Mwanaka and Daniel Da Purificacao
Logbook Written by a Drifter by Tendai Rinos Mwanaka
Mad Bob Republic: Bloodlines, Bile and a Crying Child by Tendai Rinos Mwanaka
Zimbolicious Poetry Vol 1 by Tendai R Mwanaka and Edward Dzonze
Zimbolicious Poetry Vol 2 by Tendai R Mwanaka and Edward Dzonze
Zimbolicious: An Anthology of Zimbabwean Literature and Arts, Vol 3 by Tendai Mwanaka
Under The Steel Yoke by Jabulani Mzinyathi
Fly in a Beehive by Thato Tshukudu
Bounding for Light by Richard Mbuthia
Sentiments by Jackson Matimba
Best New African Poets 2018 Anthology by Tendai R Mwanaka and Nsah Mala
Words That Matter by Gerry Sikazwe
The Ungendered by Delia Watterson
Ghetto Symphony by Mandla Mavolwane
Sky for a Foreign Bird by Fethi Sassi
A Portrait of Defiance by Tendai Rinos Mwanaka
Zimbolicious: An Anthology of Zimbabwean Literature and Arts, Vol 4 by Tendai Mwanaka and Jabulani Mzinyathi
When Escape Becomes the only Lover by Tendai R Mwanaka

a sky is falling by Nica Cornell
The politics of Life by Mandhla Mavolwane
Death of a Statue by Samuel Chuma
Along the way by Jabulani Mzinyathi
Strides of Hope by Tawanda Chigavazira

Soon to be released

https://facebook.com/MwanakaMediaAndPublishing/

Printed in the United States
by Baker & Taylor Publisher Services